THE JOURNAL OF INSECURITIES

A SHORT NOTE MADE FOR YOU

LAKSHMI AK

I dedicate this book to all those who struggle with self-doubt and low self-esteem. I want you to know that you are unique and worthwhile.

Contents

Foreword

A world that demands you to be the best simultaneously creates a parallel universe inside you that is over-flooded by social anxiety, self-doubt, inferiority and a whole new constellation of insecurities that will blind you in no time from seeing your own worth. Soon you will be lost in the constraints of time, light and all forms of life. No matter how much our heart calls out for help, the instant solutions that we get online are a far cry from what we are looking for. In today's fast-paced world when people are busy hiding their insecurities with filtered reality, I am delighted that my closest friend Lakshmi AK with whom I share all of my insecurities has penned her perspectives on insecurity, judgement, gender disparity, self-contemplation, rejections, jealousy and many more.

"The Journal of Insecurities" is not just a book, it's a monument of real-life experiences of herself and many others. Reading the book gave me the same intimacy we shared during our college days. Deeply intensified with life experiences and her own contemplation on human emotions and psychological complexities, the book addresses your caged insecurities and helps you to see the world from a different perspective. I would like to take a moment to thank Lakshmi for painting her emotions with the colours of reality and giving me a great reading experience.

Priyanka joy

Preface

I never had any plan to discuss the topic of insecurities. Everyone is aware that insecurities exist, and no one is completely free of insecurities. Everyone has walked the trail at least once in their lives. But, thinking about how insecurities control today's age, I merely wanted to make something similar. I can't influence the attitudes of every living being on the planet. My words have the chance to control the path. You make the decision to follow the path. It's difficult to talk about insecurities since no one understands how to convey them. No one knows how to fully explain it. People are worried about their insecurities, nevertheless are unable to treat them. This is the primary reason why the topic remains a hashtag.

I'd be lying if I say I've never felt insecure in my life. I had a lot of insecurities. The pattern of insecurity changed dramatically from childhood to adolescence. But, overall, I was infected. But I never thought of it as an issue to be solved back then. Today, I've figured out how to deal with my insecurities. However, many people struggle with the negative repercussions of insecurities. Many people have lost their jobs and their confidence as a result of this. I've seen many important issues highlighted in the media, but only a handful addressing insecurities. Why aren't people speaking up about it? Have you ever heard someone say, "Hey, I'm insecure now"? Does this imply that no one feels insecure any of the time? The answer is that people are embarrassed to admit they have insecurities about a few or many things. That is not an issue. Insecurity is not a crime that you have to hide the evidence. In fact, everyone feels it. It is a common feeling like anger or sadness or happy. You don't have to be afraid of that.

Nothing will go well if you don't control your insecurities. Insecurities can haunt you forever. It has the potential to undermine your accomplishment and bring you down into depression. Insecurities frequently have a negative impact on self-esteem. It has the potential to turn you into an invisible adversary to yourself. It's like poisoning your spirit and inner body by feeding your insecurities.

You may be feeling insecure for a variety of reasons. It could be your body shape or skin colour, your hair length, your sexuality or relationship outlook; it could be economical or spiritual causes. In reality, feeling uneasy is often easier than recognizing and correcting it. Yes, this is the most difficult aspect of insecurity. It can be difficult to identify or figure out why you are insecure or what is causing your insecurity feelings. It is more difficult to cure if the reason is unknown.

So the first step towards insecurity detangling is identifying it. You should have good communication with your inner self. You should know what you feel and why you feel so. Moreover, sometimes it is difficult for you to handle it alone. Communicating it with someone you trust can help. This is very important, perhaps. Try to seek help—don't be ashamed of therapy.

Even your closest friend can be a good therapist. Always keep in mind that this is not a big deal if it's under control. I want to share these thoughts that sprouted out inside my mind. This book is not to prove anything right or wrong.

I always wanted my first book to be special and worthy. That's why I decided to write on the topic that once made me suffer a lot. You don't have to expect the traditional or conventional method of an author publishing her book. This is a book that follows no rules. And the main idea behind the content itself is to go beyond the limits.

The main intention of writing this book is to provide relevant confidence to those who need it. If you are highly insecure, then go on; you are at the right place.

Lakshmi AK

Acknowledgements

I owe a debt of gratitude to many people for helping me fulfil my dreams. Above all, I was fortunate to have wonderful mentors. I'd want to express my gratitude to my parents for their assistance in the publication of my book.

I would also like to express my gratitude to all those who inspired and encouraged me to write about this topic. Furthermore, I thank my editors and designers for sticking with me throughout. This would not become a reality without your help.

Finally, I'd want to thank my readers for taking the time to read this. Thank you for taking some time away from social media to read a book. This will not let you down.

When you start accepting yourself, everything will have a
solution.

CHAPTER ONE

TO DEAR INSECURE SELF

Being secure throughout one's life is the hardest challenge. Even if one tries, many things crave to welcome insecurities. And being insecure is neither a crime nor a bad thing unless it start affecting you. By mentioning 'you', I mean your mental and physical stability. There is no such thing as a person who is born and brought up without insecurities. People consider it a terrible thing. But why so? If your insecurities are paving a way to build your strong and confident self, then what is wrong with it? Why people are afraid or ashamed to talk about their insecurities. What is it that you're afraid of?

I was born to a very traditionalist family from both my parents' sides. When I was young, I was taught many things that I followed until I was mature enough to realize and comprehend the reality behind them. With the sayings and teachings of my family members grew my traditional spirit as well as my insecurities. I lost a major part of my life feeling Insecure about each and everything. At first, I believed it was my fault. But, as time passed, I realized that insecurities are indeed a condition that plagues everyone.

Feeling insecure can be tough sometimes. But we have known many successful people who used their insecurities as their highest motivation. So the question here is, "Is insecurity a real problem?"

Many people would say that it isn't a real problem, since there are more serious problems to discuss, like the human mind and mental well-being. People are more concentrated on heartbreaks, depression, anxiety, etc. what you have to know is that insecurity has a very important role in everything that you feel and everything that you do. People find it tough to converse about since the issue is seldom thoroughly addressed. Sometimes it is being misinterpreted. An insecure mind is considered wrong. And the person who suffers insecurity is regarded as weak and poor. Society had always blamed them for not being confident and strong. But one can never be confident and strong just by flicking fingers. This will take a lot of effort. You can imagine how much society contributes to the demise of an insecure individual by preying on his fears.

The human mind is like a black hole. We haven't found out yet what is happening inside. Sometimes we are upset, and then years later we are delighted about the things that once made us unhappy. We both regret and embrace many of our great choices, as well as many of our successful mistakes. What about thoughts? It is always said that 'the more you try to forget, the more you remember it,' and it's true. This is the case with insecurities as well. The mind and insecurity are closely linked. If we can alter our mindset, we can deal with our insecurities. Perhaps, as you know, everyone is different. Everyone has a different kind of face and body. So do our minds. It's unique and it's special. We cannot predict what the other person is thinking. Similarly, we cannot compare the number of feelings they have from any emotions.

People cannot always express how sad they are. They cannot tell you what their insecurities are about. It's a common human instinct. The reactions coming out of them due to these insecurities can sometimes create serious problems like ruining a relationship. When I talk about relationships, I don't just mean romantic ones. Perhaps even a friendship can bid a goodbye.

Some people use anger and avoidance to manage their insecurities. This way of handling insecurities is yet another problem why people consider insecure beings as evil and less. Never blend your feelings. Before acting, always sort out your feelings. It can be detrimental at times. It can get much worse sometimes. Indulging your loved ones or those around you will not benefit you in any regard.

For many, it can affect their personal space of comfort and happiness. When you begin to feel insecure about anything, it gradually seeps into your thoughts. It may become a part of your life. It can change the whole mental configuration you once had. People call it maturity. But do you think there is a need for this alteration for something you were once happy for and later became insecure about? As a result, determining the elements or situations that trigger your insecurity is crucial.

Our uneasy self is an integral element of who we are. We can't afford to ignore it. But we can strive to keep it under control. We have the ability to transform it into something positive. The most important thing to learn is how to regulate one's insecure self, what to feed them, and how to properly care for them.

CHAPTER TWO

MINDFUL CONCEPT

The world had many amazing things in store for us. Just take a look around. There are many beautiful things surrounding, but we are wasting those by constantly indulging in insecure thoughts and impulses. I wish to help individuals who are always haunted with insecurities and wasting a significant portion of their life.

Before you continue reading, I'd like you to consider at least two insecurities you currently have. I want you to think about them thoroughly. Feel the tingling in your stomach, the annoyance that comes from thinking about it every time. Examine it from many perspectives. Try to comprehend it from every possible aspect. Try to address it after you've got a clear picture of it. This is referred to as the acknowledging phase. I know you're feeling bad and hopeless. However, try to feel the emotions. Begin a conversation with your insecurities. Addressing it is not an easy task. You must deal with a plethora of impulses sent by your brain, that can be either positive or negative. The same thing happens with the mind as it does with physical pain and the time it would take to heal. And the first aid you can give your mind for its ailments is to acknowledge the difficulty it faces, the real problem.

Don't worry, this has nothing to do with your personality, despite what everyone around you claims. Recognize that it is not your fault. There is no one who is perfectly secure. Every living being on our world encounters different kind of insecurities. Thus, this isn't your fault. However, doing nothing about it is totally your fault. If we take a moment to comprehend the psychology behind insecurity, we can identify it as the signals our brain is making to communicate with us. The message might be of several genres. It could be the message our brain is attempting to send us that it is afraid to do something, or it could be the threat it represents. It can also be a warning sign that our inner self is being injured in some way which need attention. How can you heal your brain if you aren't ready to understand what it's saying? However, many of us are always afraid to confront these signals since they might be painful or cause emotional suffering. As a result, people will try to bury it deep within themselves. Your insecurities will pull out stronger each time you hide it. This can lead to depression and other mental illnesses in the long run. The nervous feeling you're experiencing right now is an indication that you've been keeping something really deep hidden and denying what your inner self has to say.

I encountered many individuals who are insecure about themselves. Later I realized that everyone is some or the other way insecure about something or the other. I heard many people saying that insecurities are a part of life, so why should you bother about it. Insecurities are something that every single person wants to be free of. It could sometimes create severe issues in a personal as well as public space. Affecting self-esteem and questioning self-worth are the worst. The ultimate problem lies within the depth of any society. And in today's world, nothing changes unless and until you are strong enough to deal with it. The world, it is said, is selfish. Is it, however, the case? What is the nature of this so-called world? What created them, and how did things become so complicated?

When it comes to insecurities, the world has a significant impact on them. People say we should be strong and face it as a challenge. But was it necessary? No one else can read your mind. It's a single-code receiver system that your own mind can only crack. That is why it is being called a mystery box. No one knows what exactly is happening inside; perhaps it can control the whole body. For me, one's mind is the most powerful thing one owns. A brilliant and healthy mind can change the entire world. Similarly, being secure about the insecurity can change the entire situation.

The reasons behind insecurities are many. One can never solely figure it out. But have you ever thought about the main reason for insecurity? It's our mind itself. People later add on to it. They will poison us with the venom of negativity, body-shaming, criticisms, etc. In one way, it is their personal perspective that we don't have to worry about. But is that really possible? We have many things to concentrate on in our lives, and simply living it out for the reason of others' personal perspective is not right.

CHAPTER THREE

IS A PERFECTIONIST A VICTIM?

Everyone wants to be perfect. No matter how beautiful and adorable you are, people will always find some or the other reasons to criticize you. Being perfect is not a bad thing, perhaps being perfect solely for the sake of others is! You should be perfect for yourselves. Being flawless is not a bad thing; but, being perfect exclusively for the sake of others is! You should be perfect for yourself. Always bear in mind that dealing with the perceptions of others is not your responsibility. People will always find fault with you in one way or another.

Having trouble with your flaws is normal. There is no one without any flaws. Adding confidence to prepare an accepting and admiring mind is really important. If you move behind, following your flaws, nothing good can happen. Correcting our mistakes is not an issue, perhaps it's a good thing. Indeed, there is some difference between flaws and mistakes. Correcting your flaw for your self-satisfaction is okay, but if you do it for others or to satisfy others, then you are into trouble. It's like questioning yourself for what you really are.

If a person is really striving for flawlessness, then he is definitely the so-called perfectionist. He will constantly be working and worried about, fixating on the imperfections. Perfectionists actually gain less and attain stress. Their life will always be stressful. They will be constantly disturbed by the thought that life is always hard on them. They always concentrate and put in most of their effort and energy to create an illusion of 'what makes it perfect'. When you are able to cope with your flaws, you can actually become the best version of yourself, by yourself and for yourself. But if you put your legs in the shoes of a perfectionist, you won't be able to satisfy yourself with anything. You will be continuously laying the road for your inner self to plunge into the darkness of depression.

Not only depression, perhaps you can invite serious other troubles as well. Every small thing that happens around you will impair your mental steadiness. You will always be dissatisfied, regardless of what or how much you have accomplished in your life. You cannot always enjoy success, since each time you crave for perfection. Sleeping and eating disorders will follow you. When you try to make something perfect from one side, you are digging deep failures for other things on the other side. Investing your energy into perfectionism is a bad idea.

Whom should we blame for this? Our mindset, mostly. This isn't entirely accurate, however. There are many other factors that lead a person to become a perfectionist. No individual is born with the mindset of setting and achieving goals. Nothing inside an infant's brain is set up to identify what is perfect and what is not. It is the society and the long tradition that set up rules and norms that make him or her, victim in the first place. We have heard our teachers asking us to be perfect in everything. In many situations, they even scold us for showing or expressing our flaws. Yes, we should get corrected and guided. But do you think it is right to make someone do something they are against, which can create an insecure self-inside them?

The first tutor of a child is perhaps their parents and the surrounding. Every parent wants their children to be perfect in everything. We have seen the trend of pushing kids to study arts, music, yoga, sports, etc. Every parent wants their child to be unique. But you should remember one thing, that every single being on this earth is unique and valid.

When you force your child to be the topper, be special, or be the best, you are nurturing the comparison and competitiveness inside a child's young brain, which in the future can damage not only his life but the entire generation. Having a competitive mind is not a problem; perhaps if your competitive mind is stronger than your inner self-respect and will power; it will undoubtedly do more harm than good. Everyone deserves to feel happy for themselves. When the parents continuously compare their child or start questioning his talents or interests, They are harming a flower that is just starting to bloom by adding extra fertilizer to help it grow much faster and hence more attractive, until the caring becomes poison and kills the bud. This is precisely what happens when a youngster is applauded for doing something they are not capable of.

The other trend is for parents to continually support their children in everything they do. There is always a misconception that if a child is not properly supported and guided by the parents, they will become bad individuals in the future. Is this true, actually? Parent should guide their young ones. But, this doesn't mean providing them with anything to everything. A child wants to learn the values. The value of good and bad, the value of money, the value of recognition, and the value of accomplishing something through one's own efforts and dedication. Parents should guide them in both their failures and success. Adequate motivation is important when it's needed; if not, they will become a perfectionist. Nothing will make them satisfied.

It's a good thing to do everything perfectly. However, craving and striving for perfection is toxic to the mental self.

Being satisfied with your-self is far better than being a peer, perfect for others.

CHAPTER FOUR

SOCIETY OR SOCIAL ANXIETY?

We know that everyone depends on the society of which they are part of. Societal influences were always there, even before humans developed language to communicate. Social life and social well-being play a crucial part in our life. We cannot always stay away from society and its social norms. Really? Why can't you? There are positive as well as negative influences from society. A society can build a person as well as destroy a person. It depends on what kind of society you are really into. If you are not happy with the social life you are a part of; it doesn't conclude that you are incompetent or that you are bad; perhaps it's just not the right place for you.

We are social beings, and we cannot neglect the fact that each decision we make has a social connection. We are encountering society and its behaviours from our very birth itself. In fact, we are born into a society. After all, no one had ever heard of the phrase "socialization," which is now considered a requirement in all facets of life. Being social is considered a very good sign of character development. We have seen many parents trying to make their children socially active to gain a better impression. This is not a bad thing until we start discussing introverts.

Through its particular culture, customs, institutions, and more, our society provides us with the labels we see to categorize the people we encounter. This is the main reason behind people's judgmental approaches, which we will discuss in the coming sessions.

Being an introvert is not at all a bad thing. In fact, you have the complete freedom to be who you are and to choose what you want. Being an introvert doesn't mean that a person always sticks to his room; perhaps you can also see introverts in social gatherings and discussions. Introverts don't really love to be alone all the time, in another way, they just love the time with themselves rather than hanging out with others. They love the inner thoughts that they communicate within themselves. They like the lone time inside their house. Likewise, they like to get indulged in deep thoughts. In short, they are not against society or social activities. Such misconceptions make them identified as insecure and confident less people. This is why being an introvert is considered a bad thing.

We have seen some parents forcing their children to talk with other people. Even in schools where our primary education begins, we have seen many students forced to stand up and say the answers. Sometimes teachers even punish the students for not being loud and energetic in the classroom. They conduct many activities to change the child's inner configurations and to convert them into an extrovert. This is why extrovert students are always considered smart and talented, whereas introverts are considered weak and fragile. Sometimes these kids were even labelled useless. You don't always have to raise your voice inside the classroom to be a good student; in fact, introverts are no less than extroverts.

According to many surveys, it has been identified that half of society constitutes introverts. That means half among the billion people are asked to change who they really are to be accepted by the society. Do you think this is fair? Introverts have the right to enjoy equal freedom as extroverts are given. We cannot force an extrovert to stay in his home without social interactions; it could damage him. We have seen many news reports saying that many extroverts face hard situations and danger with their mental lives due to pandemics. If this is the case with extroverts, you can imagine how much damage we are giving to the introverts in our society. This is why many introverts face depression and social anxiety.

Being an introvert will never keep you from failing or stop you from achieving your goals. In fact, many famous personalities such as Emma Watson, Albert Einstein, Abraham Lincoln, Mahatma Gandhi, etc., all were introverts. This clearly sorts out that being an introvert doesn't mean that you are useless or less talented. If you don't want to go out and meet people, then stay home because nothing matters more than your comfort zone and inner peace. You cannot change what you really are. If someone tries to change it, correct them, and realize that you are the leader for yourself, it's your responsibility to keep yourself happy.

Extrovert or introvert, social anxiety can come anytime, irrespectively. It's normal to feel nervous in some social situations. But if you have a significant amount of anxiety in everyday interactions, then you should be aware of social anxiety. You will get nervous all the time with a high amount of self-consciousness and negative feelings. When you fear being scrutinized by society or being judged by people, you definitely have social anxiety. Once you are infected, you cannot control this, but you can regulate and slowly eradicate it. All you need is confidence and self-respect.

Social anxiety can create many mental health disorders, which can lead to depression and grief. Negative self-talk, poor social skills, low self-esteem, difficult social relationships, hypersensitivity to criticisms, suicide, or suicidal attempts are some after-effects too. In short, social anxiety is not a silly thing to get neglected. And if left neglected, it can control your life. It will affect your future and relationships as well.

There are many reasons for social anxiety. Skin colour, height, weight, body structure, hair, job, physical disorders, etc., can contribute to the reasons. Social anxiety can follow its path when society starts judging people based on skin colour or financial position. Many people try to recreate themselves to avoid these anxiety feelings. Is this right or wrong? Absolutely, it is entirely dependent on the individual. If a person feels insecure about anything, he has the right to change it. What makes it wrong is that he tries this change without being willing to conform to cultural norms.

If you wish to do a nose job or lip treatment, go for it. You should be aware of the consequences and side effects and be extremely careful. And don't do it because society asks you to do it. Do it if you feel like doing it. Some people offer motivating statements such as "respect yourself as you are" and "don't colour your hair, paint your nails, or wear makeup." From one aspect, it is very true that we should always respect who we really are. But it doesn't mean that we are forbidden to do what we like. The reason why these kinds of motivational dialogues spread out in our society is that these kinds of people consider only physical appearance to identify an individual. It is not solely the physical body that constitutes a personality, and we should also try to understand the inner self.

People who change their hair color or do tattoos to hide their scars are not always insecure. Perhaps there are many people who do so. The advice for them is that you should love your body; you can add anything that can make you confident and happy but doesn't always do this for society. Moreover, your inner self is what matters the most.

If you are nervous or uncomfortable every time in a social situation, the stress in these situations is too much to handle.

You can beat social anxiety by several methods incorporating your mental health. Avoid situations that can affect your healing process. You should also find a way to deal with your past trauma.

Try to face the situations that make you feel anxious in a positive way.

CHAPTER FIVE

NOTHING COMES IN WITHOUT A JUDGMENT

"Thinking is difficult, that's why most people judge." ~ Carl Jung

Judgment or being judged is a very serious problem many of us face. People judge us on something to everything. Sometimes they don't even need a reason to judge. People judge others because of two reasons. Firstly, they are overconfident about themselves that everything or everyone else around them feels less valued. And secondly, they feel no confidence at all. They can't accept the fact that you are better than them. There are also several other reasons why people judge others, sometimes no reasons at all.

You have no clue how much a person's life can be affected by your judgment. Sometimes judgment or being judged can make people lose self-esteem and confidence.

They even try to question themselves.

Those who feel confident and good about themselves will have less interest in judging others. Despite our best efforts, we all judge others. Imagine you were going to a supermarket or a park where you came to see a person wearing torn outfits and no shoes with messy hair. Definitely, you will get an idea that he is a poor guy, and sometimes you will offer him help, or sometimes you avoid getting near to him. This is a kind of common judgment everyone makes. We don't know whether the person is rich or poor. We don't know what his background is. But still, we judge from his looks.

Judging people by looks is a very common type of judgment. And almost every one of us will do that in some other phases of our lives. Society had made some norms and set rules of perfect physical appearances in which we all follow the path. If someone chooses a different path, we will start to judge them. We pass judgment on the most insignificant aspects of other people's lives.

This is why we have gender norms in operation. Some people have difficulty accepting a lady dressed in a men's attire. People are sometimes evaluated just because they are linked to another person. People do not always recognize they are passing judgment on others. This is the primary reason why judgmental attitudes are so difficult to remove. Judgment is a natural instinct. However, one can keep their judgmental words and thoughts from harming others. Judging is nothing more than our endeavour to establish a hierarchy of better than and less than, superior to and inferior to, and assign value to everyone and everything we encounter. We have an intrinsic need to constantly be correct, better, and superior. We tend to judge because our binary view of the world requires us to be either right or wrong.

Not only that, but we tend to make a certain concept in our mind in which it will be difficult for us to change certain patterns. That means if you're a dancer, and you are good at it, you will definitely feel less for people who can't dance. Maybe it's difficult to accept the fact that everyone is different, but you can try to cooperate by accepting others as they really are.

Yet another part that comes along to contribute to judgments is social comparison. We often compare ourselves with others. How do you know that you are not beautiful or you don't have a pretty face? These are the thoughts that affect many of us. So, who said you are imperfect? The comparison itself, when you compare yourself with others, you will start judging yourself.

This social comparison process, in which we evaluate ourselves in terms of how we compare to others, both personally and professionally, can lead to poor self-perception. Are you beautiful or unattractive? Are you a winner or a loser? Do you think you're clever or stupid? It probably depends on who you're comparing yourself to. We make the mistake of comparing ourselves to others all the time.

If you compare yourself to an incorrect reference group, you may feel ordinary, average, or inferior in terms of aptitude, competence, or attractiveness. According to research, men who compare themselves to media-idealized male physiques have an unfavourable perception of their bodies. When young women compare themselves to fashion and media models, they feel the same pressure and stress.

Aside from that, studies have discovered that people who spent more time on social media had reported a significant decrease in self-esteem. Moreover, social media itself has contributed to the platform for comparison and passing judgments.

The most essential thing to realize is that there is a significant difference in energy and outcome between seeing other people's success and utilizing that vision to encourage you is relentlessly berating yourself because you aren't where they are. If comparison makes you feel useless and depressed as if you can't have what you desire and "deserve," and you resent others for what they have, it's time to stop comparing or change your perspective on it.

Yes, if we let it, the social comparison may have a detrimental influence on our self-esteem. We are prone to comparing ourselves to others. Attempt to resist the urge. If you can't stop yourself, at the very least manage who you compare yourself to and seek out individuals with whom you compare positively, your self-concept will be more realistic, and your self-esteem will be higher as a result.

CHAPTER SIX

SOCIAL MEDIA AND SOCIAL DILEMA

We are social beings. We need to stay connected with each other for our survival. We always need adequate companionship at some or the other point in our life. Being disconnected from social interactions can cause serious problems with mental as well as social health. Many of us use social media sites like Facebook, Twitter, Snapchat, YouTube, and Instagram to locate and communicate with one another in today's society. While each has its own set of advantages, it's vital to realize that social media will never be a substitute for real-life human interaction. In order to trigger the hormones that relieve stress and make you feel happier, healthier, and more positive, you must interact with others in person. Spending too much time on social media, ironically for a tool supposed to bring people closer together, can instead make you feel more lonely and isolated—and aggravate mental health issues like anxiety and depression.

We cannot completely question the worth of social media since it has many positive sides. It helps us to get connected virtually. We can stay in touch with our family and dear ones even from long distances. Social media also provides a platform for discussion and sharing thoughts and ideas. We can reach out to as many people as with a single touch. Because social networking is such a new technology, little study has been done to determine its long-term effects, both positive and negative. Multiple studies, on the other hand, have discovered a substantial correlation between extensive social media use and an increased risk of sadness, anxiety, loneliness, self-harm, and even suicidal ideation.

Even if you are aware that the pictures you see on social media have been edited, they can nevertheless make you feel anxious about how you appear or what is going on in your own life. We're also all aware that other people only discuss the great aspects of their lives, rarely the terrible periods that everyone goes through. That doesn't make you feel any less envious or dissatisfied when you go through a friend's retouched images of their sunny beach vacation or hear about their wonderful new job promotion.

In short, social media can contribute a lot to your insecurity circle. The worst thing that can seriously injure our mental health is so-called cyberbullying. Because of the damage imposed on the victim, there is a relationship between cyber bullying and depression. A person who has been the victim of cyber bullying may become worried and lose interest in things they like. As a result of depressed episodes following a cyber-bullying incidence, sleeping patterns and eating habits, as well as energy levels, may suffer. There are instances in which the victim's brain recalls the traumatic incident, triggering a physiological stress reaction and PTSD. This occurs because the brain may secrete stress hormones on a constant basis, causing the person to repeat the unpleasant incident over and over again. This increased sensory overload can overwhelm a person, leading to a torrent of negative thoughts and a lack of emotional control.

Cyber bully victims may develop a bad view of themselves as a result of their experiences. Because the brain's defensive mechanism comes in and makes one doubt their ability, confidence and decision-making abilities are impeded as a result of the trauma. Making decisions on what meals to eat or what clothes to wear might be challenging for some individuals. This is accompanied by a generalized feeling of lethargy that prevents sufferers from getting out of bed or taking a shower. They don't even feel like doing what makes them happy. They will start questioning their worth. These kinds of insecurity causes can lead to serious mental disorders and end up the victim into depression.

When you post bad or demotivating comments on someone's post, you lose only a few words and a few seconds but imagine how much damage you are imposing on that person. Not even a thousand words can heal what you have just done. We should matter people's mental health. It is as equally as important as ours. There is nothing one can gain from making someone else insecure.

Reach out to someone if you face any kind of cyber bullying since many studies have shown that around 45% of the victims go through suicidal thoughts or self-harm. Sometimes things go beyond your control. It's not an ending; try to reach out to someone or start your healing process and make it a beginning.

CHAPTER SEVEN

DOES GENDER REALLY MATTERS?

Gender can become a serious reason for insecurities, especially for women. This doesn't mean that all women are insecure. But the gender gap and biased approach of the society can sometimes cause gender insecurities. This is not only in the case with women; perhaps some men also face the same. Their gender can be their villain.

Mental illness affects roughly twice as many women as males. This gender gap in clinical depression may be related to socioeconomic inequities and disparities in living standards among countries. Currently, these discrepancies are not reflected in health policy. Perhaps the brain configurations of men and women are different to deal with pain and stress.

There are many things in our society that contribute to gender insecurities, and the major one is gender inequality. Women were always considered weak and fragile. This might be a reason for forbidding many girls from attending school or going to work in many societies around the world.

In the name of safety and security, many rights and freedom were denied to women. They even face restrictions for wearing their choices of outfits. Sometimes society itself makes women insecure by assigning a man to look after them. Society teaches us that a woman is not safe outside without the protection of men. The opinions and ideas of women are also not considered sometimes. All these things contribute to the feeling of insecurity.

Not only this, there are several other kinds of gender insecurities. While talking about gender, the majority of us would consider only male or female. We have a tendency to neglect or ignore other types of gender. Our society finds it really difficult to accept a third gender. This is the main reason why the queer group has to face a lot of trouble with their mental health since each time society is feeding them with insecurities that can never be eradicated. If LGB persons are more likely to experience mental discomfort and disease as a result of social stress, it is critical to identify this risk as well as components that alleviate stress and contribute to mental health. Only with such comprehension can psychologists, public health specialists, and policymakers collaborate on the development of effective preventative and intervention strategies. The relative quiet of psychiatric epidemiological research on the mental health of LGB people may have been intended to minimize stigma, but it has backfired, leading to the marginalization of this critical topic.

Questioning someone's gender can also induce problems. Society had created several gender roles. And these are applicable for only two genders, so-called male and female. There are many situations where a person is forced to hide his gender identity.

Not only gender but perhaps sexuality also encounters the same issues. Sometimes it's difficult for a person to reveal his sexuality, whether he/she is gay or lesbian or bisexual etc., this fear can be categorized into passive insecurities. This is completely unacceptable since every single being has the right to live according to their wish. No one has any right to question anyone's sexuality or sexual orientation.

There is yet another trend in our society that it is considered as a shame or bad quality being a gay or lesbian. I have seen many boys getting angry when someone asks them whether they are gay. Such responses from our society and the unacceptability of many sexual theories are the reason why people feel insecure about themselves.

Transgender persons may suffer anxiety as a result of the discrepancy between their biological sex and gender identity. This can have an impact on their body image, and studies reveal that transgender persons had greater levels of body dissatisfaction prior to completing gender confirmation therapy. LGBTQ+ persons usually experience greater levels of stress as a result of stigma, prejudice, and discrimination. This 'minority stress,' which includes not just experiences of discrimination, harassment, and victimization, but also more internalized sentiments of shame, may be contributing to the LGBTQ+ community's mental health difficulties. This 'minority stress' might also be linked to concerns with body image. According to one study, having sexual relations with males who had internalized negative ideas about homosexuality and sexual orientation was connected to general body dissatisfaction, muscularity dissatisfaction, and body fat dissatisfaction. Another study comparing the body images of non-binary and binary transgender persons revealed that harassment and rejection were associated with lower levels of body admiration, as well as lower self-esteem and life satisfaction. According to our poll, 40% of homosexual, lesbian, bisexual, and other respondents were dissatisfied with their body image, compared to only 18% of heterosexual respondents.

CHAPTER EIGHT

THAT COMFORT ZONE WE OWN

We all will have that one person or few people with whom we can be ourselves, without any masks. We don't have to hide anything from them. We can be the true self of us. These kind of people with whom we feel extremely strong and relaxed are known as comfort zones. We identify comfort in them because we know that they won't judge us. We are free to share everything. Having people in your life throughout without judging you are a real blessing.

It is even good to have someone to share things with—all your deep secrets. Everything is related to your emotional realm. This comfort zone can be your boyfriend or friend or cousin or parents or anyone who could possibly embrace you. Try to hold them tight. Yes, it's a fact that people change. Not everyone accompanies you throughout your life journey. But it's good to cross paths. To have someone to make you feel proud about yourself.

The worst-case scenario is that the person whom you trust the most cheats on you. The insecurity you are going to deal with it is the worst. No matter how strong a person you are, the emotions are going to consume you. Trusting someone requires a lot of effort from your mind and soul. You trust someone, not with your brain, perhaps with your soul. Trust is something beyond the emotional realm. When you trust someone, you will expect their presence throughout your life. You expect them to be with you like the good old person they once were. As I mentioned earlier, people change. You may lose someone at the same time you'll gain another one. Its life. If you have someone consistent, then it's good for you. But having inconsistent mental relationships doesn't imply that you are weak or worthless.

It's hard to overcome the insecurities caused by our comfort zones. In other words, it is the one that's going to hurt the most. You feel like never trusting people again. You feel like you don't deserve to be loved. You will start to question your worth. You will have tendencies to hurt yourself. You will feel like nothing matters. The major problem in these cases is that you won't feel like relying on someone else to help yourself or to seek help. It will be hard for you to trust again after your heart is broken. I have seen many of my friends going through the same. I have seen how hard it is.

I know it's hard, more than verbal explanations. But you don't deserve this. Try to comfort yourself by adding positive affirmations to your inner talks. It's not your fault that people have changed or someone has changed. There is a situation and needs to check your self-confidence and identity. We all will have some or the other kind of identity. Our identity is like a bookmark in other people's life. Having a negative or positive identity for yourself is something that is totally dependent on you.

Never trust someone more than you trust yourself. And never depend on someone for almost everything.

Sometimes it is possible to get hurt so badly by your comfort zone.

Sometimes coming out of your comfort zone can bring or provide an additional growth zone for you. It's not a problem to consider leaving the comfort zone. You can step out of your comfort zone and step into your growth zone. Never regret for someone who had left us alone. Never overthink about the reasons why they left. As I mentioned in the beginning, every person has the right to choose what they really want. It's completely their decision whether to stay with you or to leave you. Sometimes even they had undergone some unpleasant events that cannot be explained. Exiting from your life would be mandatory sometimes. Excuse people for not wanting to stay in your life and let them leave.

I have seen many people forcing other people to stay in their life. I have seen people sacrificing their happiness and passion just to be within their comfort zone. This is wrong. You should never sacrifice yourself for anything else.

Allow yourself to heal. It will take a lot of effort and time. Don't give your mind the key to your life no matter what. Don't outrun thoughts without proper control. Respect other people's choices. Sometimes it's better off with you. Never forget that other people too have a life that deserves peace. Don't force someone to stay, whether it's physically or mentally. In these kinds of situations, you will be wondering how to deal with them. The only possible way is to take your time. Time has the power to heal everything. The insecurities will also leave you shortly when you learn the art of living at the fullest.

CHAPTER NINE

INNER SELF TO REJECTONS

I know it's hard to embrace yourself and motivate your inner mind to forget someone or some group of people who had accompanied you throughout your tough times. It's hard to ignore the feelings of rejection. Talking about rejection can affect one so badly that it can indulge one into a mental breakdown. When you get rejected, you will feel worthless and alive for no reason good. You feel so many emotional hazards altogether in your mind. You will even start to hate yourself. The rejection or being rejected is one of the toughest things a mind could face.

It's normal to feel so many emotions at the same time because of rejection. It can be built your insecurities into heights in which you will need to put all your efforts to defeat them. Insecurities can't be ignored. Grief can't be ignored. By pulling out these feelings, your mind is trying to get revived. It is trying to get cure for itself. But if you forbid your mind from expressing it, it can demand the worst situations. You will be overwhelmed. If you hide your feelings that your mind wants to put out away, you are injuring your inner self. You are making it harder for the mind to recover. So the first and foremost thing to do is to express your inner self. Let all your emotions flow out. Don't hide it and suffocate your mind. In the end, all you need is time.

Nothing is possible without your corporation with the time. Time is a magic healer. It can heal everything. It is a good medicine for your mind. So take your time. Start healing yourself. Imagine good things. There exists a tendency for your mind to recollect all the negative energy you have in yourself. It makes all the negative thoughts rush back into the floor. This in turn would obviously make the situation worse. Give yourself the time you need. Prepare yourself for everything, although you cannot predict future events, you can still hold an optimistic approach about it. Always feed your mind with positive thoughts. About the happy moments, you had. This is one way you can neglect all the negative energy inside you. Try to fill all the gaps and infinity thoughts you possess inside yourself. These gaps are formed because of some unanswered questions and situations you had in your past.

CHAPTER TEN

BODY SHAMING AS A JOKE

We all deserve to feel good about ourselves. How many times have people told you that you look fat? You don't have a pretty face? You are too skinny? Or you should wear more makeup to look beautiful? If it had happened to you even at once, then you are a victim of body shaming. The term "Body shaming" is a modern one that has been in practice for a long period. It occurs in various forms – subtle suggestions, discreet ideas, blistering censure, seemingly harmless hints, scathing rebuke, extremely rude comments, anonymous internet trolls, and many more. Body shaming is the after-effect of an individual's negligent judgment, thoughtless analysis, and reckless criticism of someone else on the grounds that they feel the latter doesn't fit in the mold of so-called beauty standards. Being stout, thin, short, tall, shaggy, bald, dark, fat has all been part of the never-ending reasons to be body-shamed in both cyber and the real world. Body shaming can influence a person in numerous ways. It can lead to mental trauma and negative emotional effects, comprising a lessening in self-esteem and other concerns such as eating disorders, anxiety, body dysmorphia, and dejection. Also, body shaming can lead to serious depression, especially when people feel their bodies cannot encounter social ideals. It can be associated with overweight and the disability of an individual to function normally. We can see body-shaming even in movies. In other words, movies contribute a lot to the realm of body-shaming jokes.

Movies, in general, express body shaming as a feature for focus in a dramatic line or in a comic manner to induce comedy. As follows, creating entertainment from such a critical subject can advance the public to have a mocking attitude towards people with extraordinary body size, skin color, appearance, etc., which is considered imperfect and unacceptable. Our culture loves the dogma of a "perfect body." Whether in real life, print, movies, television, or online, seeing someone who doesn't fit the matrix of beauty and identity notions is rather considered offensive to some people. While body-shaming has been in society for quite some time, the internet and social media platforms such as Instagram, Twitter, and Snapchat, have brought it to an all-time high. Technology has formulated the focus on appearance easier and conferred way to a platform that more commonly summons body shaming and bullying. They function with a critical part in the construction of selected body figures as "ideal." These notions are commenced through cinematic representations; nonetheless, the contemporary film constructions have started it in an entirely different manner, often looking into the pain and suffering apart from "mocking" fatness. Body shaming could be terribly a serious issue in our society. Not solely body-shaming and the physical look had commented on one's personality, but also the social standards to which one belongs and, therefore, the cultural identity delineates oneself. In short, we can generalize the origin of body-shaming from the history of a politically correct society. It gave birth to many ideologies for the sake of a happy and peaceful society. But the aftereffects were ironic. It formulated groups in between the society known as classes. Class differences not only affected society but the films too. Several cultures like diffident classes, social group teams, etc., were disgraced and desperately represented in quite a lot of films, whereas the high and wealthy categories were symbolized nearly as noble and acceptable. This shaped the class distinction to confront elevation and vulnerability through films.

Movies continually influence society and the approach of individuals towards each other. Whenever the films expose "fat men and women" as "ashamed" in front of society, the viewer's take it as a chance to condemn the individuals similar to the characters of the story. Body shaming materializes in many means; it is critiquing or judging somebody's appearance or commenting on their body and comparing it to other personages. When society stretches much significance to appearance, fashion and physique, the world continues to associate beauty with slimness. Someone who seems more than the supposed "actual size" is considered as "physically excessive" or "morally inadequate." Movies, as they are the filmic illustration of the concepts, commonly display the fat people as mediocre when compared to the admirable societal concepts.

Body-shaming is the practice of humiliating others because of their physical appearance; it affects both men and women psychologically and physically, and it has shifted our society's "ideal body type" for decades. The film has made an important and remarkable contribution to this.

The film is a visual art form used to stimulate expression that communicates ideas, stories, perceptions, feelings, beauty, or atmosphere by means of recorded or programmed moving images along with sound and their sensory simulations. People are influenced by movies. The most obvious example is the popularity and acceptance of film actors who play heroic characters in films. On the other hand, people do not worship the actors who play villain roles. This demonstrates how a character in the film has an impact on society. A film may deal with a wide range of topics by presenting its own viewpoints or perspectives on them. These topics are seen and conceived by the viewer through the eyes of the camera. The movie has a greater impact on society than any other medium. As a result, the contents of films that are shown to the wider population should be handled with extreme caution and care. When talking about body shaming, it's important to figure out what's at the root cause of the problem. If we dig deep enough, we can infer that lack of political correctness was the start. By deceiving people, it serves as a silent killer in society. The tool for better propagation is still a major concern, which is why ignoring political correctness in movies has such a negative impact on today's generation. It can persuade people to believe in certain things and take certain paths. Interfering with other people's personal lives, pressuring people to adhere to certain philosophies, manipulating things, and so on are all examples of political correctness, according to some movies. But in reality, this is not true. It needs to be eradicated from society. We've all admired and praised these things in the past. However, the time has come for a change. We must alter our perceptions and take a stand against these films. Time for change is not far unless society opens its eyes. Weight and body type stigma can have long-term psychological and physical health implications. People with disproportionate bodies are typically ostracized, according to recent studies.

According to studies, being body shamed throughout adolescence has both short- and long-term mental health impacts. Body shaming causes a variety of mental health difficulties, including poor self-esteem, anxiety, and depression symptoms. When people are verbally insulted, it can lead to emotions of avoidance and isolation as a result of the embarrassment they are experiencing. There is also an increase in low self-esteem, self-image, and self-worth sentiments. Worse, it can make a person feel isolated and sorry for themselves, leading to despair.

Furthermore, body shaming can lead to poor eating habits. It can go in either direction: gaining weight by eating too much or losing weight by refusing to eat. People may be at risk of developing an eating disorder as a result of this. Body shaming is unpleasant and should be avoided. Take note of how the people around you — your friends, family, and coworkers – act. If you see someone body shaming someone else, confront them and educate them. Discuss the negative consequences of body shaming in a civil manner.

No one has the right to question your worth. Even if they do so, never get disappointed and start to question your self-worth. Everyone has a different and beautiful body structure. It doesn't matter whether you are skinny, fat, or black or white. Whether you have curly hair or straight hair or no hair at all, nothing matters. What matters is your inner peace.

If you get into your head what the other people say about your body, you are going to have no benefits. Be happy with what you want and not what your society wants. You are the one who is paying your bills. You are the only person who can confront yourself. Perhaps only you can make you feel okay. Next time don't fall for some unethical logical comments that people pass over your body or your personality.

CHAPTER ELEVEN

INSECURITY INTO JEALOUSY

Insecurity can manifest itself as jealousy. Jealousy is the dread of losing something you already have, such as a friendship or a relationship. People who suffer from jealousy may frequently feel threatened by others. Even if you're not, you could feel like you're competing with others. Insecurity can lead to jealousy, especially if you have an insecure attachment style.

Jealousy is usually about people, whereas envy is usually about things. Perceiving another individual as a challenge to you or your relationships is a form of jealousy. A person who is envious may hope they have something that someone else has.

You could be jealous if your mother confides in your siblings rather than you, but you might be envious if your best friend has a finer house than you. Although both, this is a part of insecurity. Jealousy can be a result of shame. For some people, emotions of guilt — such as when you make a mistake or say something harsh — can lead to jealousy. Shame affects almost everyone at some time in their lives. Shame, on the other hand, can occasionally turn into more damaging feelings. Addressing shame might help you avoid other bad emotions like insecurity and envy. If you don't address the source of your envy or jealousy, they may potentially become toxic. These types of insecurities are very often found in marriage or love relationships. In these kinds of situations, we feel the emotions of belongings. We feel like needing them all around us. We want to hold their hands and dissolve into the world of uncertainty. But then how come the feeling of jealousy can overtake happiness? Simply because our insecurities fuel our jealousy. Jealousy is a normal feeling that arises when a person is insecure about their relationship (whether that relationship is with a romantic partner, a parent, a sibling, or a friend). Jealousy is something that everyone goes through at some point in their lives. However, issues can occur when envy transforms from a good feeling to an undesirable and unreasonable one. Excessive and irrational jealousy can lead to the end of a relationship. Learn how to cope with jealousy and insecurity in a relationship to overcome these feelings and build your connection. There's no reason to think that it'll go away if jealousy isn't handled. Optimism will not make jealousy go away. It reaches deep into one's core and has profound roots, and overcoming these sentiments requires awareness and effort. Jealousy is acceptable too sometimes, but it may be detrimental to well-being when it becomes extreme or illogical. It's critical to be able to tell the difference between good and unhealthy jealousy if you want your relationship with yourself to succeed. When jealousy is strong or illogical, the situation changes dramatically. Jealousy that is irrational or severe is frequently indicative of a potentially harmful relationship. As their emotions and concerns overwhelm them, jealous people eventually lose control of their relationships. To maintain control and soothe or mask their feelings, they may employ psychological abuse, verbal bullying, and violence.

It's normal for couples to conflate healthy, fleeting jealousy with love. Normal jealousy, on the other hand, is far from loving. The individual who is jealous grows increasingly afraid, angered, and dominating nature causing chaos in the relationship.

Over time, jealousy can turn into bitterness and defensiveness. It also undermines trust in a relationship and leads to more disputes, especially if the jealous person makes continual demands and questions the other person. Physical difficulties might arise as a result of intense emotional events. Trembling, dizziness, melancholy, and sleeping problems are all physical signs of envy. Their persistent rage and need for reassurance can also lead to the breakup of a relationship, particularly if they become aggressive and do not deal with their jealousy in a healthy way.

If you're experiencing jealousy, you should address it as soon as possible before it escalates. You and your partner could find healthy strategies to deal with jealousy together.

Not only with romantic relationships, but even a friendship can also be destructed with unwanted jealousy. Feeling jealousy is not at all a problem. It's a normal and common thing among human beings. But you have to know where to set the limits. If jealousy is ruling your life and your decisions, you are really into trouble.

CHAPTER TWELVE

THE BOTTOM LINE

It's normal to have days when you don't feel like doing anything. Constantly questioning yourself, on the other hand, may have a negative impact on every aspect of your life, from your physical health and mental well-being to how well you perform at work. Being unsatisfied with your love relationships may be quite hazardous since it makes you more vulnerable to stress and jealousy. Not only does it have an influence on you, but it also has an effect on others. According to research, your self-esteem influences how content you and your partner are with your relationship. There are methods to boost your self-esteem if you have the appropriate knowledge. While it will not happen immediately, with the right skills and mentality, you may begin to change the way you feel about yourself. If you're always chasing after other people's goals while neglecting your own, you're not respecting yourself enough. Adding in more self-care in your everyday recurring aid you to battle poor thoughts and build up your self-worth. The next time you feel ashamed or self-conscious, try to laugh it off. It's easy to berate ourselves when we slip or make a mistake. However, beating yourself up because you didn't receive that huge promotion or missed a crucial phone call traps you in a vicious loop of shame and self-loathing. Use the following tactics to combat negative ideas when they arise: Forgive yourself and recognize that these are isolated instances that do not define you. Make a list of your negative thoughts so you can easily evaluate them when you take a step back. Consider what you've learned from the expert, and then return your attention to the positive. Consider the times when you've felt extremely insecure. What were you doing? What were you up to?

Noticing the people and things that deflate your ego can help you identify what to avoid. If you surround yourself with so-called "friends" who make a practice of pointing out your weaknesses, it's a clear hint that you should seek out better company. Celebrate your accomplishments and speak up after you've had a big triumph at work. Although it may look strange at first, being satisfied with what you accomplish may have a significant impact on your self-esteem. On some level, everyone experiences a lack of confidence; but, if uncontrolled, it may have a substantial influence on your everyday life. Building up superficiality isn't always simple or quick, but the ultimate result is well worth it. Don't be scared to seek assistance if you believe you may benefit from it. So, what are the attitudes or actions that shape this internal critique? Sort it out and redefine yourself.

Take your time to heal yourself. You don't have to prove anything to anyone. The moment you realize its importance, you will never have to face insecurities.

CHAPTER THIRTEEN

HEAR THEM OUT

SPEAKER A:

I always wanted things to be perfect in this imperfect world, that's how I was brought up. I was taught that if you're less perfect, you won't be considered as one among us!

Since then, I have been conscious about my physical appearance, the way I speak to people, the way I present myself, the way I walk, talk, eat, etc. I always wanted to be slim, but I didn't know that I was good the way I was; nobody made fun of me or insulted me because of my physical appearance, just that I wanted to be in perfect shape. I had all these small consciousnesses in my mind about physical appearance or maybe desire to be slim. Later I got married and everyone told me transparency is the key to a successful married life, so I started sharing all my insecurities one by one with him. I thought he would understand, but it turned out to be a huge mistake! He started using these insecurities against me. He made me more and more insecure about my physical appearance. He even started comparing me with both his and my friends, family, and neighbours. Not only that, but he tormented me because I was not physically appealing to him. It reached an extent where I was unable to go out thinking I was not good enough. It's not your fault that you're born in this way, but it becomes your fault if you allow someone to take advantage of you. If you're in the right place, it is easy to overcome your insecurities. You don't get to choose the situations all the time, but you can always decide whether this is good for you or not, if not! Do not spend another minute just running away from the darkness; it is never too late

Insecurities do not develop as it is; there is always a reason behind every insecurity. Find them, analyze them and think whether it's worth spending too much time thinking. If the creator created this way, definitely there's a reason, happy with whom you are. And it's always your choice that matters, your happiness that matters. People would say ill about you no matter whatever or how much you try, just do not take them if it doesn't do any good. Find positivity in everything you come across. Hardship should make you stronger and bolder cause there is so much yet to come. Life is a combination of both positive and negative events. Do not get drowned in your insecurities because there is so much to explore in this world, and do not let some bad experiences hold you back.

SPEAKER B:

Insecurity is actually a lack of self-confidence or fear of being bullied or left out because of some aspect of oneself that one feels is not good enough. But even before one fully understands what the definition of insecurity is, every child in our society brought up in our norms feels insecurity to full depth in their flesh and bones as some unexplained fear or worry. They feel it even before they know what it is. That was exactly how things were for me. It can be any part of our lives. Unfortunately, things to feel insecure about oneself never run out. It can be as simple as the way we laugh for some of us, while it can be the way we look for some others.

I have always felt insecurity and comparison as two sides of a coin. You can toss it and get a head, but the tail is right under it. Or you got a head because the tail went under. Similarly, you feel insecure about your body because comparison is still active under your thoughts. A sense of better or worse arise only when you compare things with something else. It is impossible to eliminate comparison in many aspects of our lives, but maybe in some cases, the conclusion can be 'different' instead of 'better' or 'worse.' I still remember that day in college when all of us were dressed and happy for an event. That's when one of my friends came over and told me that I looked really beautiful, and that compliment made me happy for a few seconds actually. Because she continued with, "...but you would look even better if you had curves like your roommate." I remembered dialogue from a famous show, "Everything that someone said before but is horseshit." The best way to describe the feeling I had is someone stabbing my throat and chest simultaneously. For one moment, I wondered it was even a compliment or an insult.

The body is not the only thing that could become a potential point of insecurity, at least in my experience. Although for most of us, the very first encounter with insecurity is related to body imaging and body shaming. A few other examples could be the accent, homeland, work, income, etc. For me, another crazy insecurity was my name. It was not a rare name, but people keep pronouncing it wrongly, and some of them familiar with the name are like. "I thought that was your nickname. Is that really your name?" Every time somebody points out something like this, I seriously think about changing my name even when I like it. When it comes to insecurity, it has mostly been people pointing out something about you that you barely found an issue with, and that's where it begins. For a very long time, I thought the problem was with people. But it is the social conditioning that makes people think it is "cool" or "progressive" or "friendly" to make people insecure by passing these "friendly and polite" comments. Later I realized that it is actually people trying to outrun their own insecurity. Maybe that gives them a sense of being "better" perhaps. Even if we didn't start this idea, not trying to change it and instead of complaining about it is not at all a fruitful approach. The simplest step of doing it is changing the way we conclude our thoughts, as I mentioned before, from "better" or "worse" to "different," and trust me, that makes a difference, not in every level but at least some of it.

SPEAKER C:

Being a queer member, I had to face many situations in which sometimes I even felt worthless. I hated my life as well as myself for many years; when I saw kids of my age enjoying with their parents, all I had was dramatic and cruel memories of my parents and relatives forcing me to behave like a boy. I was born a boy. And that wasn't my choice. If everyone in this world enjoys freedom, why it's forbidden to some people or in some situations? All I wanted in my entire life was freedom. I wanted to express myself as who I am and not what my parents wanted me to be. I felt really insecure about myself. I felt worthless. I even had thoughts about hurting myself. I cried all night to sleep. Sometimes it hurt me like something punching on my heart. The pain was more than I could ever bear. I remember people insulting me and torturing me. They blamed me for being who I am. No one ever accepted me. It took me a lot to realize what the solution was. You don't have to be afraid of anything else in your entire life. Be who you really are and who you really want yourself to be. Everything else is secondary. It took many years for my family to accept me. I would have never become who I am now if I had given up. So my advice is, never let your insecurities consume you. Love yourself the way you are.

SPEAKER D:

Until a few years ago, I was never insecure about anything. I had a very difficult childhood. I had no one with whom to discuss or address my difficulties. But I was content with myself. Later, I became involved in a relationship that consumed me. At first, it was a very happy relationship. We were both glad. I started telling him everything. After a few months, it began to cause complications in our relationship. He began to blame me for who I am. He was not prepared to recognise how vulnerable my mental feelings were. But, once again, I adored him and was willing to go to any extent for him. He struck up a conversation about other girls one day. He began comparing me to othersHe gently drew me into sadness. I was completely self-conscious. He was quite helpful to me in numerous ways. This is why I couldn't leave him. He started with emotional blackmail. After much struggle, I was eventually able to exit the relationship. It was quite difficult for me to say goodbye to him. I was devastated by the separation. We suddenly met again after a few years. He began to show concern for me. He asked me to be his best friend. It was a good friendship until some other factors intervened. It was against my morals.I decided to take a break, and it was only then that I realised I was falling back in love with him. I had no idea he was that nasty. Furthermore, I've never been the type of person that makes someone stay in my life. I've always respected other people's decisions. I told him I had feelings for him. He flatly refused me. That's when I realised he'd been faking his feelings for the past few months.It shattered my heart. Someone pretended to be in love, and you completely fell for it. It was quite painful. It took a long time for me to recuperate. I began to doubt my own worth. I even despised myself for being unlovable. But gradually, I became aware of the toxins that e had put into me. My mind is now cured. I understand what I'm saying. I accept his apology. I adore and love myself. I am no longer insecure. I want you to be happy and deserving of yourself. Don't let anyone ruin your joy.

57

Reference

Sheri Stritof. (2022, February 24). *How to Deal With Jealousy in a Relationship.*Verywell Mind. https://www.verywellmind.com/overcome-jealousy-in-your-marriage-2303979

The Weight of Words: Effects of Body Shaming on Mental Health. (2022, February 8). Mind Shift. https://www.mindshiftwellnesscenter.com/the-weight-of-words-effects-of-body-shaming-on-mental-health/

Body image, sexual orientation and gender identity. (2020, August 6). Mental Health Foundation. https://www.mentalhealth.org.uk/publications/body-image-report/sexuality-gender-identity

VisweswaranBalasubramanian @MyCosmos Jan 03, 2021, 20:35 IST. (2021, January 3). *The Real Reason we Judge Other People (&What it Says about Us).* Times of India Blog. https://timesofindia.indiatimes.com/readersblog/mycosmos/the-real-reason-we-judge-other-people-what-it-says-about-us-28804/

Robinson, L. (2022, March 3). *Social Media and Mental Health.* HelpGuide.Org. https://www.helpguide.org/articles/mental-health/social-media-and-mental-health.htm#:%7E:text=However%2C%20multiple%20studies%20have%20f

Caprino, K. (2017, August 18). *When Comparing Yourself To Others Turns Self-Destructive.* Forbes. https://www.forbes.com/sites/kathycaprino/2017/08/18/when-comparing-yourself-to-others-turns-self-destructive/?sh=47fa26606539

K. (2020, March 20). *Self-Esteem: What About Social Comparison?* Kit Welchlin - Welchlin Communication Strategies. https://welchlin.com/self-esteem-what-about-

REFERENCE

social-comparison/

Be strong and support your inner self who is suffering...

61